That which does not kill us makes us stronger.

T0089337

✧ Friedrich Nietzsche ✧

TAURUS

April 20–May 20

LILY

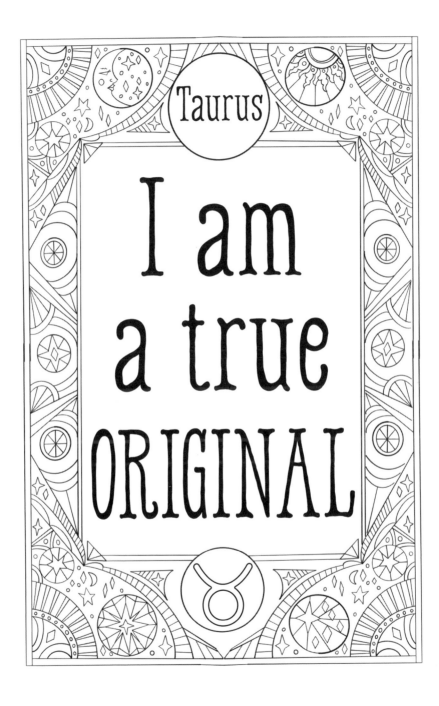

Taurus

I am
a true
ORIGINAL

spring

Taurus

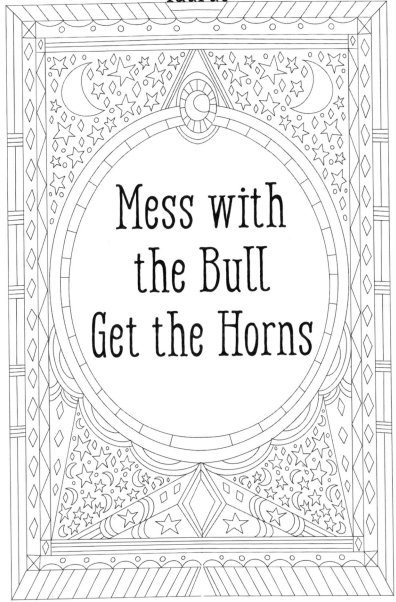

Mess with
the Bull
Get the Horns

Taurus

Ruled by Venus

Creative

DETERMINED

Loving

TOUGH

LOYAL

RULING HOUSE

2

The House of Value

TAURUS

✧

My work makes a true difference

✧✧✧

TAURUS

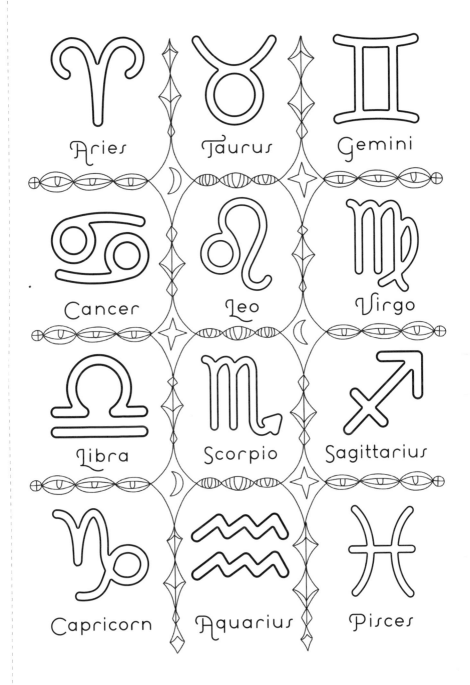

Aries

Taurus

Gemini

Cancer

Leo

Virgo

Libra

Scorpio

Sagittarius

Capricorn

Aquarius

Pisces

Earth Signs

Taurus

Virgo

Capricorn

LET THE STARS LEAD THE WAY

Image by Andrea Lauren © Simon & Schuster, Inc.